Cocktails for Survival:
Not as trump as you drink I am

By Drunk Publius

First Published in the United States of America in 2017
by Driveway Designs, LLC.

Find us at trumpedupdrinks.com

ISBN-13: 978-0-692-82643-0

Library of Congress Cataloging-in-Publication Data is available.

DRIVEWAY
DESIGNS
EST. 2016

Drunk Publius

COCKTAILS FOR SURVIVAL
Not as trump as you drink I am

By Drunk Publius

"These are dark times, there is no denying.
Our world has perhaps faced no greater threat than
it does today. But I say this to our citizenry: We, ever
your servants, will continue to defend your liberty
and repel the forces that seek to take it from you!"
Rufus Scrimgeour

A BRIEF WORD ON HOW TO USE THIS BOOK:

Alcohol has a long and important history in human society. So does humor. This book is an effort to harness the power of both to create some joy out of a mostly joyless situation. But, as Spiderman told us many, many times, "with great power comes great responsibility." Please use this book responsibly. It's all fun and games until someone blacks out, gets alcohol poisoning, or operates heavy machinery under the influence. Don't do any of these things. If any of these drinks looks like a bad idea, it probably is. When in doubt, we encourage you to laugh at the jokes, use your common sense, and skip the drinks. Thank you.

The Drunk Publius family

Table of Contents

Chapter 1: Shock

Chapter 2: Denial

Chapter 3: Anger

Table of Contents

Preface

The week after the 2016 election, a group of friends came together to have a few drinks and commiserate about the state of the nation. This event was called "Drinks in the Driveway."

We sat in the driveway, had a few drinks, and started talking about how we were going to get through the next four years. Someone suggested alcohol and humor. We all laughed, and the idea for this book was born.

Warning

We do not advise alcohol as a solution to your problems. Humor is an acceptable solution.

Do not consume more alcoholic beverages than you can safely drink, and don't drink and drive.

Chapter 1

SHOCK

shock
SHäk/
noun

1) a sudden upsetting or surprising
event or experience.

"It was a shock to watch the election
results on November 8th, 2016."

OR

"I feel shocked." Pepper Brooks

BUT NOT

"Chaka Khan, let me rock you. Let me rock
you, Chaka Khan." Melle Mel.

THE PENCE

Oh, this drink looks totally innocent. It looks downright reasonable compared to the other drinks. It knows how the game is played. It knows all the players. It has leadership experience. It's probably doing all the actual work from behind the scenes. It looks like it would be a better option than The Trump (page 25). But be careful. Be very, very careful. Hoosiers* know what kind of damage The Pence can do when you're not watching it very, very carefully. One minute, The Pence will be nodding at you with its "more in sadness than in anger" look of disapproval, the next you'll be required to notify the government about any menstrual irregularities you might be experiencing.

INGREDIENTS

1 cup of club soda on ice
Rohypnol (optional)

INSTRUCTIONS

Pour a cup of club soda over ice. Become distracted while someone makes an Impeachment (page 24). While you're distracted, have someone slip you a Mickey. When you wake up, your reproductive rights and marriage equality are long gone.

Serve with Ritz crackers, in honor of Indiana Superintendent of Public Instruction, Glenda Ritz, who was Pence's first victim.

*We are Drunk Publius, a shadowy, lurking figure with no fixed address, not some chumps from Indiana.

THE FLAG BURNER

On November, 29, 2016, the actual president-elect of the actual United States of America tweeted the following:

"Nobody should be allowed to burn the American flag - if they do, there must be consequences - perhaps loss of citizenship or year in jail!"

To preserve your freedom of expression, your citizenship, and your liberty, we suggest that you burn the following instead.

INGREDIENTS

1 part Campari liqueur
1 part white creme de cacao
1 part 151-proof rum
1 part blue Curaçao

INSTRUCTIONS

Pour the Campari into a clear glass. Using the back of a spoon to slow the flow of the liquid, layer the blue Curaçao. Vigorously shake the white creme de cacao and rum in a shaker and gently pour on top of the blue Curaçao. Set the drink on fire with a lighter. But don't you dare garnish this with a tiny flag on a toothpick, because that'll get you in hot water.

Tastes great with the tears of citizens weeping because the actual president of the actual United States of America, a man who has pledged to stand up for "Article 12" of the Constitution, has no functional understanding of the Bill of Rights.

"I don't know the scientific explanation, but fire made it good." Homer Simpson.

THE PUTIN'S PUPPET

The latest in Russian puppetry is unpresidented. This drink is murky, yet disturbingly effective. Best enjoyed in a dark room alone with your laptop as you troll American websites, forums, and private emails trying to hack an election.

INGREDIENTS

2 ounces of your favorite Russian vodka

1 ounce coffee liqueur

heavy cream

INSTRUCTIONS

Add vodka and coffee liqueur to glass over crushed ice, then top with heavy cream.

"No puppet. No puppet. You're the puppet.
No, you're the puppet." Donald Trump

Pairs well with the Russian Cyberattack (page 70).

THE POPULAR VOTE

This is two for the price of one, and must be made in the presence of a group. Make The Red State (see page 62) and The Blue State (see page 79) and have everyone vote. Whichever drink gets the least votes, everyone has to drink. Throw away the other drink. Get angry if anyone suggests that the more popular drink might have been better.

Sorry, the Green drink (page 58 - Third Party) didn't get enough support to participate.

THE SMALL-FINGERED VULGARIAN

Masculinity can be so delicate. It can be threatened by pink shirts, fancy coffee drinks, or even quiche. You might put on a brave front with your locker room talk and your sexual assault, but in truth your fragile ego is hiding just beneath your thin, orange skin.

"My fingers are long and beautiful, as, it has been well-documented, are various other parts of my body." Donald Trump

INGREDIENTS

¼ of a lime

1 ounce spiced rum

1 ounce hot sauce

1 ginger beer

10 cocktail weenies

INSTRUCTIONS

Juice lime into glass of ice. Add rum and hot sauce and gently stir with a cocktail weenie, which you can then either eat or use as a garnish. Fill remainder of glass with ginger beer and enjoy.

Serve in narrow glass to accommodate wee little fingers and enjoy while snacking on cocktail weenies.

OCTOBER SURPRISE

Surprise birthday party, Shanghai surprise, "the shocker" . . . who doesn't love a good surprise? Still, some surprises can be disruptive and unpleasant. While not so deadly as the gales of November when they come early, the ratfuckery of October can do a lot of damage during election season. Whether it's an email non-story that commands three above-the-fold New York Times stories in one edition; disclosure that a leading candidate may have been lying for years about illegal arms sales; or false claims of imminent peace in Vietnam; you'll probably need a drink as you contemplate the idea that elections are decided by fickle, low-information voters who can be persuaded to ignore months or years of history and react to the latest headline when casting their votes.

INGREDIENTS

2 ounces of vodka
½ a lime
5 ounces of ginger beer

INSTRUCTIONS

Squeeze the lime juice into a mug or glass and then toss the remainder of the lime in as well. Add the vodka* then top with the ginger beer.

Garnish with mint leaves.

*Feel free to use hog manure instead if anyone says something negative about vodka while you're making the drink. That would be a surprise.

THE LOCKER ROOM

The locker room: a place where manly men can do manly things with other men. Leave the toilet seat up. Relish manly scents and crude behavior. Talk about The Pussy Grabber (see page 42). Have other men not call you a sex offender.

If you can't drink straight testosterone, we recommend The Locker Room as the next best thing.

INGREDIENTS

2 ounces brandy

1 ounce cointreau

1 ounce freshly squeezed lemon juice

INSTRUCTIONS

Mix brandy, cointreau, and lemon juice in a shaker with ice. Shake thoroughly and strain into the manliest glass you can find.

For those times when you need to appear a little less rough around the edges, rub the rim of the glass with a lemon and dip in sugar before pouring your drink.

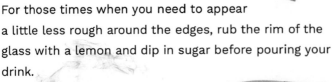

THE BIGLY

This drink is not small (unlike your hands). This drink is big. It's YUGE (see page 31). Look, grammar is hard. Forget about vocabulary. You need a big drink to deal with the 2016 election results. A drink that's so big, it's bigly. Is that a word? It is now and it's presidentially approved.

INGREDIENTS

1 bottle of sweet red wine

1 cup blueberry liqueur

1 cup raspberry liqueur

3-4 cups lemon-lime soda

2 cups frozen blueberries

lemon slices and mint for garnish (optional)

INSTRUCTIONS

In a large pitcher, combine red wine, blueberry liqueur, raspberry liqueur, lemon-lime soda, and frozen blueberries. Stir. Add straw. This drink is big, but it's made just for you and not to be shared because sharing is for socialists.

THE MICHELLE

Michelle and Barack Obama were raised with many of the same values: That you work hard for what you want in life, that your word is your bond and that you do what you say, that you treat people with respect. This drink embodies all of these values. This drink will pass those values on to the next generation. The only limit to the achievements of this drink is the strength of your dreams and your willingness to work for them.

INGREDIENTS

2 ounces Cognac

1 teaspoon orange Curaçao

½ teaspoon fresh lemon juice

1 dash Angostura bitters

INSTRUCTIONS

Cut a lemon in half. Pare the full peel off half and sqeeze the juice from the lemon. Prepare a glass by moistening the rim with lemon and dipping it in sugar. Combine all ingredients in a shaker with ice, shake and strain into glass. Optionally, add 1 small cube of ice.

THE MELANIA

Melania and Donald Trump were raised with many of the same values: That you work hard for what you want in life, that your word is your bond and that you do what you say, that you treat people with respect. This drink embodies all of these values. This drink will pass those values on to the next generation. The only limit to the achievements of this drink is the strength of your dreams and your willingness to work for them.

INGREDIENTS

2 ounces Cognac

1 teaspoon orange Curaçao

½ teaspoon fresh lemon juice

1 dash Angostura bitters

INSTRUCTIONS

Cut a lemon in half. Pare the full peel off half and sqeeze the juice from the lemon. Prepare a glass by moistening the rim with lemon and dipping it in sugar. Combine all ingredients in a shaker with ice, shake and strain into glass. Optionally, add 1 small cube of ice.

THE SUCKER PUNCH

Nothing makes a red-blooded REAL American so mad as one of those libs with their liberally liberalness. They just won't recognize common SENSE!!! And they're always talking. With their "facts" and their "well-reasoned arguments." So smug. They're wrong, of course, but those eggheads make everything so damned confusing. And it makes a guy ANGRY. REALLY ANGRY. Especially when one of them shows up at your safe-space rally.

The Sucker Punch honors those brave Americans who will slug a smarmy Lib when security is escorting him out of the rally and he least expects it!

INGREDIENTS

12 pack of cheap beer

1 ¾ liters of vodka

2 - 12 ounce cans of frozen pink lemonade concentrate

INSTRUCTIONS

Pour the 12 pack of beer into a large container. When it stops foaming, add the vodka. Then stir in the lemonade concentrate. Pour individual servings into cups with ice. Expect the unexpected.

Chapter 2

DENIAL

de·ni·al
dən' nīəl/
noun

1) the action of declaring something
to be untrue.

"Republicans are in denial about climate change."

OR

"Trump is in denial about losing the popular vote."

THE IMPEACHMENT

Like a lot of drinks, the Impeachment seems like a good idea at the time. After a Putin's Puppet (page 14), half a dozen Twitter Beefs (page 29), and maybe a Pussy Grabber or two (page 42), you figure an Impeachment sounds like just the thing. But when you wake up with The Pence (page 12) and a pounding headache, you'll be having second thoughts.

INGREDIENTS

1 bottle peach schnapps
1 bottle mint vodka
mint leaves

INSTRUCTIONS

Pour schnapps and vodka into a bucket with all the mint leaves you can find. Set it on fire. Then, when it's too late, realize exactly what you've done, and feel deep, unrelenting dread for the future. Kiss your reproductive rights goodbye.

"The point is, you can never be too greedy." Donald Trump

THE TRUMP

You've had a rough day of Twitter ranting and reality TV show firings. Saturday Night Live is making fun of you, and you're grossly unqualified for your job. This drink is for you. It'll not only quench your thirst, but it'll build up your tolerance for more attacks from those crazy liberals who demand a qualified leader for their country.

INGREDIENTS

1 ½ ounces vodka

¾ ounce triple sec

¾ ounce orange juice

Cheetos

wedge of grapefruit

INSTRUCTIONS

Crush Cheetos. Dip shot glass rim in orange juice and then in crushed Cheetos.

In shaker filled with ice, add all three liquid ingredients. Shake, strain into Cheeto rimmed shot glass. After swigging shot, suck on grapefruit to enhance sour face.

Take a photo to post on Twitter, #cocktails4survival.

"One of they key problems today is that politics is such a disgrace. Good people don't go into government." Donald Trump

THE HOMOPHOBE

Enjoy this drink as you reminisce about the good old days, back when rainbows were hints about the weather, Liberace was merely a snappy dresser, and your marriage wasn't being endangered by the gays! This drink will make you happy and FAAAAABULOUS!

INGREDIENTS

2 teaspoons simple syrup
1 teaspoon water
2 dashes bitters

1 ½ ounces bourbon
1 orange slice
maraschino cherry

INSTRUCTIONS

In a whisky glass filled with ice, pour simple syrup, water, and bitters. Stir gently and pour bourbon over the top. Garnish with orange slice and maraschino cherry.

Pairs well with wedding cake but not pizza.

IMPORTANT NOTE: Do not set this drink on fire. Things that are flaming make you tingly and uncomfortable.

"There can be no discrimination against gays. I'm against gay marriage. I took a lot of heat for that." Donald Trump

THE THANKS OBAMA

Let's say you are the worst communist ever, and the stock market has more than doubled under your watch. Firearm ownership is at such high levels, it's almost like you weren't even "trying" to grab their guns. Your death panels are a joke. It's only natural that you want to distract your Leftist supporters from those failures and make the lame-stream media forget about your Kenyan birth. Unfortunately, we can't give you a beautiful wife, an even temperament, casual cool, or a delightful family. But, maybe you can dazzle them with this blue, Hawaiian-style drink.

INGREDIENTS

¾ ounce light rum

¾ ounce vodka

½ ounce blue Curaçao

3 ounces pineapple juice

1 ounce sweet and sour mix

INSTRUCTIONS

Mix well and serve in a tall glass. Chase with a Long-Form Birth Certificate (page 32).

"An 'extremely credible source' has called my office and told me that Barack Obama's birth certificate is a fraud." Donald Trump

THE WALL

You are back at your neighborhood tavern. You have a wicked hangover from when you were here last night, the night before, and, let's face it – pretty much every night since your wife left you for being an abusive asshole. There is a Latino guy in the corner you haven't seen before minding his own business. You are broke, feeling lousy, and that attractive lady at the bar has no interest in you. It's probably the Latino guy's fault for some reason. The only thing that will make you feel better is The Wall. Line 'em up, drink 'em down, and make yourself great again. No money? No problem. Put them on the Latino guy's tab.

INGREDIENTS

1 shot Irish cream
½ shot rum
½ shot lime juice

INSTRUCTIONS

Take two shot glasses, put one full shot of Irish cream in one and fill the other shot glass with half rum and half lime juice. Pour the Irish cream into your mouth but do not swallow. Then put the rum/lime-juice mixture into your mouth. Swish the combination around in your mouth until your problems are gone. Rinse, repeat.

THE TWITTER BEEF

Afraid to talk to people in person? Has the untrustworthy media been twisting your words? Is diplomacy dead? Need a place to prove your point with some fake news? This drink will fuel your anger while you sniff your way through angry 3 AM tweets.

INGREDIENTS

1 ounce Southern Comfort peach liqueur
1 ounce sloe gin
1 ounce orange juice

INSTRUCTIONS

Mix all ingredients in shaker with ice. Shake until well-chilled. Pour into glass and serve. Garnish with a side of beef jerky.

TIP: This drink is best served after watching the latest episode of Saturday Night Live.

"My Twitter has become so powerful that I can actually make my enemies tell the truth." Donald Trump

"Thanks - many are saying I'm the best 140 character writer in the world. It's easy when it's fun." Donald Trump

"Somebody said I'm the Ernest Hemingway of a hundred and forty characters." Donald Trump,

THE YOU'RE FIRED

Some men just want to watch the world burn. And it's tough to blame them in a country where "economic anxiety" is offered as an explanation for the election of an alleged billionaire famous for firing people on reality television. So, serve this drink in a gold goblet and light it up. Don't drink too much, though, these ingredients can get pricey, and you no longer have a job.

INGREDIENTS
1 ounce vodka
1 ounce blue Curaçao
3 ounces lemonade
splash 151-proof rum
pinch of cinnamon

INSTRUCTIONS

In your goblet, pour vodka, blue Curaçao, and lemonade. Stir well. Top with splash of rum. Light on fire. Sprinkle with cinnamon. Warning: cinnamon will spark.

Blow out flames or wait for them to die out before consuming. Be sure the goblet has cooled because you no longer have health insurance nor a way to pay for hot goblet-induced medical expenses.

THE YUGE

yuge [yooj] adj. Used to emphasize the enormity of something or someone; most often used in a braggadocious manner to gloat about oneself in hopes that no one notices your tiny hands. (Syn. bigly. See page 19.)

This drink should be made only in yuge quantities so we recommend having a yuge gathering otherwise you may end up with a yuge headache.

INGREDIENTS

⅓ cup sugar

⅓ cup water

2 ½ cups orange juice

1 cup bourbon

1 cup triple sec

½ cup lemon juice

3 cups lemon-flavored sparkling water
any leftover fruit you have around the kitchen

INSTRUCTIONS

Create simple syrup by mixing together sugar and water in a microwave-safe container. Microwave mixture for 2 minutes then allow to cool. In a pitcher or large bowl, combine simple syrup, orange juice, bourbon, triple sec, and lemon juice. Throw in fruit. Mix well. Right before serving, add sparkling water.

THE LONG-FORM BIRTH CERTIFICATE

It doesn't matter if you were born in Kenya or Hawaii, this drink is sure to whet the thirst of any right-wing conspiracy theorist. Drink more than two or three and you may not remember in which state or country you were born. No matter how many of these you offer, your guests will never be satisfied. So keep 'em coming!

INGREDIENTS

½ ounce vodka

½ ounce dark rum

½ ounce gin

½ ounce tequila

½ ounce triple sec

1 ounce sweet and sour mix

1 ounce cola or soda

maraschino cherries and lemon

INSTRUCTIONS

Fill a cocktail shaker with ice. Pour vodka, rum, gin, tequila, triple sec, and sweet and sour mix over ice; cover and shake. Pour cocktail into a tall glass and stir in cola. Garnish with cherries and lemon.

TIP: Enjoy while listening to Lee Greenwood's "God Bless the USA," or Ee Mungu Nguvu Yetu (Google it.)

THE CLIMATE DENIER

The drink industry will tell you that the evidence is inconclusive, but 97% of scientists agree that this drink is cataclysmically delicious. It will flood your taste buds with flavor and drown your sorrows. It will rise up in your glass and destroy not just your mind but maybe even those of your kids and your grandkids.

INGREDIENTS

12 ounces light rum

12 ounces dark rum

10 ounces grenadine

10 ounces fresh orange juice

10 ounces fresh lime juice

3 tablespoons sugar

1 orange, cut into wedges

a few crazy straws

INSTRUCTIONS

Mix all the ingredients in a tall pitcher or large pot and stir to dissolve the sugar. Pour into a punch bowl and add orange slices.

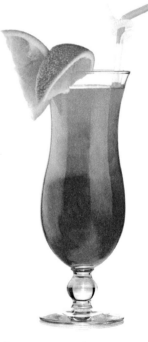

Serve this drink hot, and if people suggest that it's warm insist that "EVERYTHING IS FINE!" while clinging to your guns and Bible. Serves 10 to 12

TIP: Serve with a lump of coal, a side of fracking and a shot of despair. Pairs well with The Chinese Hoax (page 35).

"It's freezing and snowing in New York – we need global warming!" Donald Trump

THE 400-LB HACKER

This drink is an ode to both fat-shaming and hacking, all rolled up in one. When the DNC gets hacked, the only real people to blame are those with high BMIs. Who else would have the stamina to sit around the house all day (and we do mean *around* the house) on their computers, stealing confidential emails and sending them to WikiLeaks? You'd never catch a thin person getting off their treadmill in order to interfere in an election - and certainly NEVER a Russian. (*wink* *wink*)

INGREDIENTS

ice cubes
2 ounces sweet and sour mix
1 1/2 ounces vodka

1 1/2 ounces apple schnapps
maraschino cherries

INSTRUCTIONS

Shake sweet and sour mix, vodka, and schnapps in a shaker with ice to combine. Add a maraschino cherry or two to the bottom of a martini glass, if desired.

Strain mixture as you pour into glass and serve immediately.

Best enjoyed sitting in a seedy bar while bragging about your next data dump and arguing about which Linux distro is superior.

THE CHINESE HOAX

The inscrutable Chinese are to be admired for their wall-building prowess and the way their cheap, slave-labor steel holds down the price of luxury hotel construction. But we are too smart to fall for their global warming hoax. We will not be tricked into improving our environment. We will be as cunning in sniffing out their schemes as we are in designing our drinks.

INGREDIENTS

1 ½ ounces coconut rum

½ ounce creme de banana

⅛ ounce grenadine

1 ounce pineapple juice

½ ounce Midori

orange wedge and cherries

INSTRUCTIONS

Mix everything but the Midori in a tall glass and pour the Midori slowly down the middle. Or you can just blend it all together. Garnish with a orange wedge and cherries.

"The concept of global warming was created by and for the Chinese in order to make U.S. manufacturing non-competitive." Donald Trump

THE PERRY

As if 2016 wasn't weird enough, Trump wasn't the only candidate to have a history with reality TV. Even if, from time to time, he forgets the name of the Department of Energy, we must never forget that Rick Perry, Serious Presidential Candidate, was a contestant on Dancing With The Stars during the election... a novel campaign strategy, to be sure.

INGREDIENTS

1 ½ ounces gin
¾ ounces applejack
¼ ounce lemon juice

1 - 2 dashes grenadine
1 egg white
maraschino cherry

INSTRUCTIONS

Combine all ingredients in a cocktail shaker. Shake hard. Step-ball-change. Shake again. Two-three-four. Now turn! Fill shaker with ice and shake some more. Shake it like you mean it! Chasse. Chasse. Turn, turn, reverse. Cha Cha. Do the Hustle. Strain into cocktail glass. Free spin. Point finger in air. Garnish with cherry. Get eliminated.

"Oh, man, come on, this is crazy good. This is as good as it gets." Rick Perry

THE COMEY

The Comey is that drink you have at the end of the night that turns an otherwise pleasant outing into a disaster. You know the one. The evening is winding down. You've had several drinks with friends, shared a few laughs, and you're sporting a cool buzz. It's last call, and you don't want the night to end. So you have another drink for some reason. It's pointless, and no good can come from it.

Before too long, you're arguing bitterly with your friend about the merits of cursive. You're sure the guy at the end of the bar is looking at you funny. A tattoo might be cool. You think maybe bars stay open later across the state line.

When you regain consciousness, a blinding headache is about your best case scenario. You could just as easily be in a bathtub full of ice in Tijuana missing a kidney.

This is: "The Comey."

INGREDIENTS

1 ½ ounces absinthe
4 ½ ounces champagne

INSTRUCTIONS

Pour absinthe into champagne glass. Top with champagne.

Chapter 3

ANGER

an·ger
'aNG ə r/
noun

1) a strong feeling of annoyance, displeasure, or hostility.

"She's very angry that Trump is going to be the president."

OR

"Trump is angry because his chins are too big."

THE LYIN' TED

We all have those days when no one wants to be around us, and even our children are dodging our affectionate gestures. If your dad assassinated JFK, if you have to shut down the government, or if you simply have a punchable face that not-even-a-daughter could love, here's the drink for you!

"Lyin' Ted Cruz just used a picture of Melania from a shoot in his ad. Be careful, Lyin' Ted, or I will spill the beans on your wife!"
Donald Trump

INGREDIENTS

1 shot of good Cuban rum
1 shot of Canadian Club Whisky
sour mix to taste

INSTRUCTIONS

In a cocktail shaker, combine equal parts Cuban rum and Canadian Whisky with ice. Shake until your own people no longer want to vote for you. Pour into a rocks glass and float sour mix on top. Drink until you look like Pee Wee Herman's less-cool older brother or Grandpa Munster's scary younger brother.

This cocktail is terrible, but in hindsight it looks practically reasonable.

NASTY WOMAN

Oh you, with your "facts" and your "research" and your "unprecedented experience." You with your policies and your platforms. You are well prepared for the job, and you'll do it well. You are ready and able to shatter the ultimate glass ceiling, and you're going to do it all backwards and in heels. You, my dear, are a Nasty Woman. And this is your drink.

INGREDIENTS

12 ounces cheap red wine
ice

INSTRUCTIONS

Pour cheap wine into a plastic tumbler while tears of anger and frustration rim your eyes. Try not to think about the pervasive sexism that prevented you from taking your rightful place in history. Twice. In fact, it's probably better if you make at least two of these. But whatever you do, please don't subject yourself to a third!

Best served while watching SNL reruns from 2008 and 2016

NOTE: If imprisoned, pruno can be substituted for cheap red wine.

THE PUSSY GRABBER

Are you looking for the perfect drink to serve on tour buses, at pageants, and in locker rooms? Look no further. This modern variation on the old "Sweet Pussy" will have you grabbing everyone by the junk in no time. Everyone you serve this to will be talking about it for a couple of weeks, but they'll be back to talking about emails and Benghazi before you know it.

INGREDIENTS

1 part coconut rum

1 part sour raspberry pucker

Billy Bush (optional)

2 parts lemon-lime soda

2 parts pineapple juice

INSTRUCTIONS

Pour ingredients over ice in a cat mug and stir. Meow!
Does not pair well with The Locker Room (page 18).

THE LATE TERM

These almost never happen. Really. These very, very rarely happen. And when they do, it isn't like someone said, "Oh, I'm going to wait 37 weeks to have an abortion because I'm SOOOO busy." No. When these happen it is horrible and tragic, and it shouldn't have anything at all to do with politics (or humor, frankly). But here we are. And apparently this is one of the many awful political footballs we are going to bash into the ground. Fine. Here's how you deal with it.

INGREDIENTS

one ounce of cranberry juice
one gallon of vodka

INSTRUCTIONS

By the time we get to 2020, it's likely that we won't have any reproductive rights left at all. Your best shot at an abortion will be to mix the above ingredients and drink until you have a Bloody Wherever (see page 50). Maybe your unwanted child will have the sense to abandon ship. Because God knows that safe, legal abortion is off the table.

(Please don't actually try to drink your way out of an unwanted pregnancy. This is a joke. Besides, the conservatives would say that drinking is what got you into your condition in the first place.)

THE ABSTINENCE

Are you trying to avoid drinking a Late Term (see page 43)? Then this is the drink for you. And if your spouse or significant other voted for Trump, may we humbly suggest that you practice this for the next four years? Because they totally deserve it. You know that's true if you're reading this.

INGREDIENTS

alcoholic drink of your choice
one aspirin tablet

INSTRUCTIONS

It doesn't matter what you're drinking, as long as you drink it with an aspirin between your knees.

"Back in my day, they used Bayer aspirin for contraceptives. The gals put it between their knees, and it wasn't that costly." Republican mega-donor Foster Friess

"I will buy all of the women at Georgetown University as much aspirin to put between their knees as they want." Rush Limbaugh

THE POISONED SKITTLE

"If I had a bowl of Skittles and I told you just three would kill you. Would you take a handful? That's our Syrian refugee problem." Donald Trump Jr. (also known for his role as the preppy villain in every 80s teen movie).

Apparently ignorant tweeting is hereditary! Oh Don, unlike Soylent Green, Skittles aren't people. And even if they were, most decent people would eat huge handfuls of Skittles, hoping they could save as many as possible before one of the three poisoned ones killed them, you heartless monster. Try to pull the silver spoon out of your ass long enough to notice that other people have lives more complex than a piece of candy you can buy at any gas station!

INGREDIENTS

1 bag Skittles

1 bottle vodka

INSTRUCTIONS

Throw out all but three of the green Skittles, because apparently they are poisoned. No, really, the green ones will make your infused vodka taste awful. Put the remaining Skittles into the bottle of vodka and let soak for as long as you can wait. Then taste the crazy while you enjoy your sweet humanitarian vodka straight over ice, or mixed with soda. Pairs well with kebab.

"Skittles are candy; refugees are people. It's an inappropriate analogy." Mars, Inc.

EXTRA EVIL BRAND
VODKA
FLAVORED FOR ENEMIES

THE PRIVATE SERVER

We're sorry, this recipe was stored on a private server in our basement and has been deleted. You can keep searching for it. You can check back here repeatedly. You can talk about it until you are blue in the face. You can launch an expensive, and ultimately fruitless, congressional inquiry. But it's gone forever. You won't even find it on Anthony Weiner's laptop. (Caution: strong prophylactic vaccination and hazmat suit recommended if handling Anthony Weiner's laptop.)

THE ALT-RIGHT

You might need a dose of liquid fortitude when dealing with the Internet trolls from the "alt-right." Freedom-hating libs might claim that "alt-right" is a nice way of saying "racist." But, the term can cover a spectrum from alabaster Men's Rights Activists to ivory Pick Up Artists all the way to eggshell White Nationalists and baby powder White Supremacists.

INGREDIENTS

2 shots grain alcohol

8 ounces of lemon-lime soda

Pour over ice, stir, and enjoy.

Because the "alt-right" itself is so variable, ingredients for this drink are optional so long as the drink is pale and violent.

THE FUCKFACE VON CLOWNSTICK

You don't know where you're going if you don't know where you've been. That's why heritage is important. It's no secret that the new president's grandfather changed his name upon coming to America. And yet, the man who would lead us refuses to embrace his Von Clownstick heritage. Sad!

That doesn't mean the rest of us should turn our back on the rich Von Clownstick legacy. Fred Von Clownstick came to this country with little more than the clothes on his back, a dream that his family would one day refuse to rent high-end real estate to minorities, and a delicious drink recipe he named after his grandson. We recommend that the Fuckface Von Clownstick be enjoyed over the holidays with family, but, really, it's good anytime.

INGREDIENTS

2 bottles of red wine
cinnamon sticks
1 teaspoon of whole allspice
8 whole cloves
1 tablespoon orange juice
½ teaspoon ground cinnamon
½ cup of sugar

INSTRUCTIONS

Heat wine over low to medium heat (do not boil). Stir in allspice, cloves, orange juice, ground cinnamon, and sugar. Continue to heat until the sugar dissolves. Serve in a mug garnished with a cinnamon stick.

"Did you know Donald Trump's birthname is Fuckface Von Clownstick?" The Great Jon Stewart

THE TAX EVADER

If you're smart enough to avoid paying your taxes, then you likely are living quite high on the hog. After all, you didn't get rich by writing a bunch of checks. Only the best will do, and everything is classier with gold. You like to see gold everywhere you look and your choice of drink is no exception.

INGREDIENTS

½ ounce Goldschlager cinnamon schnapps
½ ounce butterscotch schnapps

INSTRUCTIONS

Mix ingredients in an incredibly expensive and fancy-pants shot glass and serve.

TIP: With all the money you save after claiming a $916 million loss and not paying taxes for 18 years, treat yourself to something special, a few gold bars or a solid gold chalice (or twenty) to make this luxurious drink even more indulgent. Go ahead, you deserve it!

"I know our complex tax laws better than anyone who has ever run for president and am the only one who can fix them." Donald Trump

"HALF of Americans don't pay income tax." Donald Trump

"I will absolutely give my [tax] return, but I'm being audited now for two or three years, so I can't do it until the audit is finished, obviously." Donald Trump

Donald Trump on not paying taxes: "That makes me smart."

"Part of the beauty of me is that I am very rich." Donald Trump

BLOODY WHEREVER

This drink is equally delicious whether you have blood coming out of your eyes or out of your 'wherever.' This cocktail will temper the rage that is induced, not by PMS, but by pro-life politicians and their ridiculous need to control your uterus. Drinking the Bloody Wherever will help you forget about all the unborn children with a right-to-life but without any other rights, public education, or adequate healthcare.

INGREDIENTS

¼ cup tomato juice

3 ½ ounces vodka

1 teaspoon Worcestershire sauce

¾ teaspoon horseradish

3 dashes hot sauce

pinch of salt

1 dash black pepper

¼ teaspoon lemon juice

1 stalk celery

2 olives

1 stalk asparagus

lemon and lime wedges

INSTRUCTIONS

In a tall glass, stir together tomato juice, vodka, Worcestershire sauce, horseradish, hot sauce, salt, and pepper. Fill glass with ice, then pour mixture into second glass. Pour back and forth a few times to mix well, then stir in lemon juice.

Garnish with two olives to represent your fertile ovaries, a celery stalk cut into the shape of an IUD for the birth control you can no longer get, and a stalk of asparagus for complete male domination. You can also suggestively dress the glass with a lemon and lime wedge, but if your drink is raped, it's your own fault.

Once completely intoxicated, turn on the TV and try to root for Megyn Kelly for as long as you can stand it.

THE MAN BABY

Have you ever heard the man baby cry?
Let us guess the reasons why

Because you've irritated your orange thin skin,
Or do you hate that huge, unflattering double chin-chin

Because your feelings are hurt over a comedy skit,
Or because every tweet proves you're a stupid twit

Is it the teeny tiny pussy-grabbing man hands,
Or the lack of intelligence that your name brands

Because you think your daughter is really, really hot
And the rest of the world thinks leave her alone, you ought

Whatever the reason, this drink is sure to ease your pain
And make the rest of this country forget their president is vain

INGREDIENTS

1 part vodka
2 parts lemon-lime soda
1 part pineapple juice
splash of grenadine
lemon slice

INSTRUCTIONS

Combine first four ingredients in a shaker and pour over ice and add lemon.

TIP: Garnishing with whipped cream, sprinkles, and a Ring Pop will pacify even the biggest of man babies.

THE LITTLE MARCO

The Little Marco is a refreshing citrus drink and is perfect for those days when you are sweating like a human man sweats. Make the Little Marco by the pitcher or by the glass, but be careful - this drink isn't for lightweight chokers - drink the Little Marco too fast, and you'll find yourself speaking Spanish and tweeting insults in no time!

TIP: Try substituting tonic water for club soda if you prefer your Little Marco on the bitter side. Best served in a short glass.

INGREDIENTS

29 mint leaves

½ lime plus 4 lime wedges

4 tablespoon sugar

1 ½ ounces of white rum

½ cup club soda

1 cup ice

INSTRUCTIONS

Crush mint leaves while tweeting and until unrecognizeable.

Squeeze juice from ½ lime into shaker, add rum and ice, and shake until you are weak on immigration and in favor of amnesty.

Place mint leaves in glass and top with lime wedges. Pour rum mixture into glass and drown sorrows.

TRUMPLE THINSKIN

nce upon a time there was a very bad hombre who wanted to be ~~king~~ president. The bad hombre lied to the people and told them that if he were president he would turn all of their problems into gold. The people believed him and elected him as president of the most powerful country in the world. No one got their gold and everyone died.

The End.

INGREDIENTS

vodka
blood of your enemies

INSTRUCTIONS

Pour into ridiculously ostentatious martini glass, mix well and drink.

Human sacrifice optional.

A tasty substitution for enemy blood can be made with Spicy Hot V8. Pour while conjuring evil thoughts.

THE HELL TOUPEE

We understand that attacking a man's physical appearance is hitting below the belt, but Trump isn't a man. He's a troll-haired monster who has a hole in his soul where his daddy's love and approval should have gone. Because of this abomination, the entire country is going to have hell to pay. And it isn't going to be pretty.

INGREDIENTS

one part champagne
one part very stout beer

INSTRUCTIONS

Pour ingredients into chilled glass and spend the evening watching your favorite late night comedy shows.

"People are constantly attacking my hair. My hair is just fine." Donald Trump

"As everybody knows, but the haters & losers refuse to acknowledge, I do not wear a 'wig.' My hair may not be perfect but it's mine." Donald Trump

"Maybe he should ease into this ... by running for a lower office first, like President of the Hair Club for Men." Jimmy Kimmel

"People are not attacking your hair, they are defending themselves from something that appears like it's about to attack them." The Great Jon Stewart

THE SNL

You may be missing Jon Stewart (page 80), but at least you still have the good people of Saturday Night Live to make fun of things that need to be mocked. Political satire is where SNL really shines: Aykroyd's Nixon, Chase's clumsy Ford on to Carvey's George the Elder ("wouldn't be prudent!"), Hammond's Clinton ("I. Am. Bullet Proof.") and Fey's Palin ("I can see Russia from my house!") Now, a toast to Alec Baldwin's spot on portrayal of Trump. SNL will always be there for you . . . or will it?"

INGREDIENTS

1 ounce whisky
1 bottle of orange Bacardi Breezer (or orange soda)
apple slice
lemon slice

INSTRUCTIONS

Mix both in a tall glass with ice. Garnish with a slice of lemon and a few slices of the Big Apple. Mock the Trump administration with brazen effrontery - for as long as you can.

Chapter 4

BARGAINING

bar·gain
'bärgən/
verb
gerund or present participle: bargaining

1) negotiate the terms and
conditions of a transaction.

"Dear God, I'll do anything to wake up and
find out this is a dream."

OR

"Daniel Webster: Oh, come, come now. Just
because you sold your soul to the devil that
needn't make you a teetotaler."

THE THIRD PARTY

When you're sick of all the other drinks and their polarized BS, you really want another choice - a better choice! You can't go wrong with this sweet, green drink!

INGREDIENTS

3 parts green creme de menthe

3 parts white creme de cocoa

1 part heavy cream

ice

INSTRUCTIONS

In a glass that no one has heard of, and that isn't even on the ballot in some states, combine the first three ingredients. Add ice. Try not to think about the fact that you're depriving the country of the opportunity to enjoy the one well-qualified, sane drink in this whole entire godforsaken thing. At least you drank according to your conscience. Jerk.

Drink until you forget basic geography, can't name a single world leader, sing folk songs and start thinking anti-vaxxers might have a point. Oh, and/or own an exotic tiger or ten.

Garnish with mint leaves.

THE PANTSUIT

Fashionable. Powerful. Independent. The Pantsuit is exactly the drink you need when preparing to debate your enemies, and you want to be strong as well as feminine; confident as well as humble.

This drink is best prepared ahead of time, for those who find preparation important to life's biggest events.

INGREDIENTS

2 ounces of your favorite cabernet sauvignon wine
2 ounces of vodka (not Russian brand)
1 ounce simple syrup
freshly squeezed lemon juice

INSTRUCTIONS

Add all ingredients to drink shaker filled with ice. Shimmy and smirk for approximately 30 seconds before straining into tall highball glass with fresh ice. Garnish with mint leaves, a cherry, and drink while preparing to destroy your opponent.

"You know what else I prepared for? I prepared to be president." Hillary Clinton

THE FAITHLESS ELECTOR

Ah, hope. It's what few had left, and what some were clinging to as they desperately searched for some shred of possibility that the unthinkable had really happened.

Hamilton wrote that the electoral college would be a guard against the election of an unqualified candidate with "talents for low intrigue, and the little arts of popularity." Hope was the last thing left in Pandora's Box and what a desperate electorate clings to when trying to push away the unimaginable.

Sadly, however, there is no basis for placing faith in a faithless elector. Lose your last shred of hope while you drink this delicious martini.

INGREDIENTS

2 ½ ounces gin
½ ounce dry vermouth
½ ounce olive brine

INSTRUCTIONS

In drink mixer filled with ice, add all ingredients.
Stir and pour carelessly into a glass.
Garnish with despair.

THE ZOMBIE-EYED GRANNY STARVER

When Paul Ryan guts Obamacare, slashes Social Security, and hands you a voucher to replace your Medicare, you'll want to toast him for giving you the dignity of grinding poverty instead of the shame of the statist social safety net that served the Greatest Generation and the Baby Boomers so well. Freedom, as the song says, is just another word for "nothing left to lose." Raise a glass to freedom with the Zombie-Eyed Granny Starver.

INGREDIENTS

1 ounce white rum

1 ounce golden rum

1 ounce dark rum

1 ounce apricot brandy

½ ounce 151-proof rum

1 ounce pineapple juice

1 ounce papaya juice

dash of grenadine

INSTRUCTIONS

Shake everything but the 151-proof rum. Add optional lemon slice and pour into a tall glass over ice. Add the 151-proof rum. Then light it.

The Zombie-Eyed Granny Starver pairs nicely with a can of beans heated over a garbage fire.

THE RED STATE

Does the willful destruction of our environment, our institutions, and our country have you seeing red? Do men in white sheets and confederate flags get you excited? Do you long for a bygone era that never actually existed? Invite all your friends to a grand old party and serve up this conservative cocktail.

INGREDIENTS

¾ ounce lemon juice

¾ ounce simple syrup

1 ½ ounces whisky

3 ounces Mike's Hard Cranberry Lemonade

INSTRUCTIONS

Mix lemon juice, simple syrup, and whisky in a rocks glass. Scoop in ice. Top with Mike's Hard Cranberry Lemonade. (Cranberry juice can be substituted for Mike's Hard Cranberry Lemonade.)

If you're feeling a little liberal, garnish with fresh cranberries and a lime.

CAUTION: Side effects may include marginalizing minorities, assaulting women, fearing gays, whining about the good old days, and yelling at kids to get off your lawn.

THE BAD HOMBRE

"We have some bad hombres here, and we're going to get them out."
Donald Trump

If the bad hombres from Mexico are as exceptional as this drink is delicious, then we don't want to be good. Mr. Trump, tear down this wall!

INSTRUCTIONS

Invite all of your hombres over for tacos and beer. Rapists and drug dealers, optional.

"I love Hispanics!" Donald Trump

"My culture is a very dominant culture, and it's imposing and it's causing problems. If you don't do something about it, you're going to have taco trucks on every corner." Latinos for Trump founder, Marco Gutierrez

THE CONVERSION THERAPY

This fabulous therapy drink has been known to Prevent Excessive Nonsense and Conservative Extremism. Traditionalists recommend heating this drink with electro shock currents, but we find this harms the flavor and ruins the drink. We think it's fine just the way it is.

INGREDIENTS

1 ounce vodka

½ ounce peach schnapps

1 ounce cranberry juice

1 ounce orange juice

INSTRUCTIONS

Fill an extra large glass with ice. Pour peach schnapps, vodka, cranberry juice, and orange juice into the glass. Enjoy this cock tale while imagining Mike Pence in drag. Pairs well with The Homophobe (page 26).

DISCLAIMER: This drink has been proven to be completely ineffective by actual psychotherapists, although it will get you drunk. But you don't need a psychotherapist to tell you that.

THE HAMILTON

If you're a bastard, orphan, son of a whore, or a Scotsman you'll love this drink. Enjoy while publishing persuasive anonymous essays that move a country of voters to your side, suiting up to battle the British, or having an affair while your wife is on a visit to her father. Two hundred years later, you can write a book of drink recipes.

INGREDIENTS

¾ ounce sweet vermouth

2 ½ ounces bourbon whisky

1 dash bitters

1 maraschino cherry

1 twist orange peel

INSTRUCTIONS

Mix the vermouth, bourbon whisky, and bitters with a few ice cubes in a mixing glass. Stir gently so the spirits don't get their feelings hurt. Place the cherry in a nicely chilled cocktail glass and strain the whisky mixture into the glass. Rub the edge of the orange peel over the rim of the glass and place it over the drink. Just don't put the peel all the way in, you're still straight that way.

TIP: Raise your glass to freedom and try and figure out how to get all those who #BoycottHamilton on Twitter to give you their tickets to the most fantastic musical of all time.

"The cast and producers of Hamilton, which I hear is highly overrated, should immediately apologize to Mike Pence for their terrible behavior." Donald Trump

THE WOMAN CARD

Fighting for women's health care, paid family leave, and equal pay for equal work is frustratingly difficult, especially when many men are trying to thwart you at every turn. We recommend you reduce your stress with this drink while you prepare yet another strategy to attempt to make the world realize that women are people. Unlike corporations, who we already know are people.

INGREDIENTS

1 ½ ounces gin

¾ ounce fresh lemon juice

¾ ounce simple syrup

champagne

INSTRUCTIONS

Add gin, lemon juice, and simple syrup to a shaker filled with ice. Give a little shimmy and then strain into champagne flute. Fill glass rest of the way with champagne. Garnish with sugar coated lemon peel.

THE FILIBUSTER

Let's be honest. The next couple of years are going to take more than mind altering amounts of alcohol. It's going to take grit, endurance, and stamina to get through them. This entry is not so much a drink recipe as a training regimen. You can do this one in solidarity with your favorite senator as he or she faces down the majority which will, no doubt, forget about the electoral college and howl sanctimoniously about the glories of majority rule.

INGREDIENTS

100 beers

100 miles

1 week

INSTRUCTIONS

The challenge is to run 100 miles and drink 100 beers in one week. You will probably want to work up to this one (or skip it altogether). Do you spread the beers and the miles out evenly over the week? Front load the miles and backload the beers? It's up to you. Like navigating the Byzantine rules of the Senate filibuster, therein lies the game!

Chapter 5

DEPRESSION

de·pres·sion
dəˈpreSH(ə)n/
noun
1) feelings of severe despondency
and dejection.

"After the 2016 election, we all started drinking
liberally to feed our depression
about the direction our country is going."

OR

"The size of Trump's baloney caused her
to feel a deep depression."

THE RUSSIAN CYBERATTACK

Uh oh! You have just looked at email that doesn't belong to you, and you've exposed systemic favoritism! You're about to get fired, drop out, or move to an embassy for refuge! You may have even skewed the results of an entire election! It's probably the fault of this drink...but it's not your fault. Nothing is ever your fault. It's rigged.

INGREDIENTS

1 ½ ounces vodka

5 grapes

1 teaspoon brown sugar

splash of soda

INSTRUCTIONS

Mix grapes and brown sugar in a shaker and spear phish them with a spoon until they're a compliant pulp. Add vodka and shake. Pour into Moscow Mule glass and add a splash of soda.

Pairs well with Putin's Puppet (page 14) and borscht.

THE NOTORIOUS RBG

You can't spell "Ruth Bader Ginsburg" without "gin," so it's only fitting that a drink in her honor should feature it prominently. And what is more vintage, more timeless, than the humble gimlet? All you need is gin, lime, and a hint of sweetness, just like RBG herself. Both hail from the 1930s. Both have a bit of a pucker to them. Both tell it like it is.

INGREDIENTS

At least 1 part excellent gin
1 part Rose's Lime Juice

INSTRUCTIONS

Combine in a shaker with ice, shake for at least four more years, if there is a god, and pour into an old and sturdy tumbler with a lime wedge. This drink needs to be strong. Really, really strong. We're all counting on The RBG to be as strong and healthy as possible for as long as it takes to get a Democrat into the presidency. Then it can retire. Maybe.

Drink while defending women's rights and being tired of still having to fight the same old misogynistic bullshit after all these years.

"I can't imagine what this place would be - I can't imagine what the country would be - with Donald Trump as our president."
RBG

THE BASKET OF DEPLORABLES

Hey, we all have deplorable people in our lives. WE CALL THEM FAMILY MEMBERS! (Thank you. I'll be here all week. Try the veal!) You can't pick your family, but sometimes you have to give them a gift. Have no fear! When in doubt, a gift basket is always a great option, and this one is sure to please the White Nationalist in your life. Perfect for Easter!

NECESSITIES

one small to medium sized Confederate flag

one large bag of Cheetos or several snack sized bags

as many napkins as you can find

one large wicker basket

6 pack cheap beer

INSTRUCTIONS

Line a basket with the symbol of treason, racism, slavery, and failure. In it, arrange the cheap beer and Cheetos and tie with a red or black ribbon. After arriving at party, give everyone a napkin. A Basket of Deplorables is perfect for the deplorable person you pulled in the family gift exchange!

> "You can choose your friends but you sho' can't choose your family, an' they're still kin to you no matter whether you acknowledge 'em or not, and it makes you look right silly when you don't."
> Harper Lee, *To Kill a Mockingbird*

THE SUPREME COURT

When the Supreme Court renders voting rights, environmental protection, reproductive freedom, and "justice" into nothing more than fond memories, remember that it was made possible by Senate abuse of the advice and consent clause following the death of Justice Scalia. The Senate failed to act on President Obama's nominee for a year. If you have a year to sit around and do nothing, we suggest you combat strong-arm political tactics with a strong drink.

INGREDIENTS

one shot vodka - Kennedy

one shot light rum - Thomas

one shot gin - Ginsburg

one shot triple sec - Breyer

one shot peach liqueur - Roberts

one shot amaretto - Alito

one shot grenadine - Sotomayor

a dash of sweet and sour mix - Kagan

a splash of beer - Zombie Scalia

INSTRUCTIONS

Add first seven ingredients to a glass with ice, top off with the last two ingredients and stir.

Bonus: Do a shot every time the Senators who blocked Merrick Garland sanctimoniously declare that a president's nominee deserves an "up or down vote."

THE HOT DAUGHTER

"Don't you think my daughter's hot? She's hot, right?" Donald Trump

A drink that brings a whole new meaning to 'keeping it in the family.' This drink is really something, a beauty.

INGREDIENTS

2 ounces of your favorite whisky
(we suggest a nice bourbon or scotch)
1 tablespoon honey
10 ounces hot water (hot tea is a nice substitute as well)
1 teaspoon lemon juice

INSTRUCTIONS

Put hot water into mug and microwave for 1 minute until really hot but not boiling. Add whisky, honey, and lemon juice. Stir until honey and common decency are completely dissolved.

"She does have a very nice figure. I've said that if Ivanka weren't my daughter, perhaps I would be dating her." Donald Trump

"I would never buy Ivana any decent jewels or pictures. Why give her negotiable assets?" Donald Trump

CROOKED HILLARY

What to do with a woman who has the audacity to defy conservative social conventions? Why you investigate her, of course! You dig up all the dirt you can (and create some when you can't) to show people how corrupt she is. Benghazi. Clinton Foundation. Deleted emails. Private server. Wall Street speeches. White House looting. The JFK assassination. Covering up the truth about Area 51. The Moon Landing. Crystal Pepsi.

We told you she was crooked! Lock her up!

INGREDIENTS

2 ounces bourbon

1 ½ ounces grapefruit juice

½ ounce maple syrup

2 ounces ginger beer

INSTRUCTIONS

Mix bourbon, grapefruit juice, and maple syrup in a shaker with ice. Shake thoroughly and strain into a cocktail glass. Top with ginger beer.

Be forewarned! Consumption may cause you to walk as crooked as Hillary is.

THE CABINET APPOINTMENT

Without ever having spent a day in office, Trump has appointed:

- A labor secretary who doesn't believe in minimum wage.
- An education secretary who doesn't believe in public schools.
- An attorney general who doesn't believe in civil rights.
- An EPA administrator who doesn't believe in climate change.
- A secretary of state with ties to Russia.
- An energy secretary that wants to scrap the department.
- His children to high-level government positions.
- An interior secretary who supports fracking on public lands.
- A treasury secretary who worked for Goldman Sachs.
- A transportation secretary married to a Washington insider.
- A health & human services secretary who opposes the Affordable Care Act.
- A commerce secretary that wants to impose steep tariffs on China.
- A secretary of Housing and Urban Development who has said he does not want to work in government and believes the pyramids were used as grain silos.

What's next? Walmart's president for head of the Small Business Administration? Putin himself for secretary of Homeland Security? Kanye West as Minister of Humility? Cruella deVille for Secretary of Canine Relocation?

Enjoy this ironic drink as the Trump administration destroys everything they can possibly get their hands on.

INGREDIENTS

craft beer	flannel
Buddy Holly glasses	vinyl records
(to wear, not to pour into)	

Dress up like your favorite hipster and drink your craft beer while wearing your Buddy Holly glasses and looking snidely on everyone else. After all, hipsters love irony, and we figure someone ought to be enjoying this disaster.

"I drink," [Fortunato] said, "to the buried that repose around us."
"And I to your long life." The Cask of Amontillado (it's ironic, look it up)

THE BIDEN

They can take away our health, our wealth, our clean air, our rights, and screw up our country in so, so very many other ways. But they can never take away our memories of Joe Biden. Diamond Joe. Uncle Joe. The coolest vice president ever. The man who launched a thousand memes. To honor Joe, you want a drink that makes you feel happy; a drink for the man who has suffered more grief than any 10 people should experience and just keeps on keeping on, smiling, laughing, loving, and generally being a badass. We're going to go with something simple and cool with this one.

INGREDIENTS

1 ounce lime juice

1 ½ ounces vodka

1 teaspoon powdered sugar

INSTRUCTIONS

Stir the ingredients with ice, strain into a cocktail glass. Garnish with lime or lemon peel ribbon.

Pairs well with The Thanks Obama (page 27).

"The American people have not become heartless." Joe Biden

THE BLUE STATE

Feeling blue? Time to get social. Get your friends and neighbors together and throw a progressive party. Drinking liberally is half the fun, especially since depression is covered by Obamacare.

INGREDIENTS

1 ounce peach schnapps

1 ounce blue Curaçao

2 ounces vodka

6 ounces lemon-lime soda

INSTRUCTIONS

Mix peach schnapps, blue Curaçao, and vodka in a tall glass. Scoop in plenty of ice. Top with soda.

Use caution when consuming. You don't want to end up sleeping with a conservative which could lead to needing a Late Term (page 43).

"The biggest divide in this country is not between Democrats and Republicans, it's between people who care and people who don't." Rachel Maddow

"This political climate today reminds me of what my father must have gone through in 1942, when the winds of war and fires of hate were surrounding him. We have a candidate for the presidency of the United States, Donald Trump, using the same rhetoric that my father must have heard from elected officials." George Takei

THE GREAT JON STEWART

> "I heard a joke once: Man goes to doctor. Says he's depressed. Life seems harsh, and cruel. Says he feels all alone in threatening world.
>
> Doctor says: 'Treatment is simple. The great clown - Pagliacci - is in town. Go see him. That should pick you up.'
>
> Man bursts into tears. 'But doctor...' he says 'I am Pagliacci.' Good joke. Everybody laugh. Roll on snare drum. Curtains." Rorshach

Throughout history, it has been the jester who could best speak truth to power. In our time, Jon Stewart has been that jester, skewering political blowhards and members of the media who gave them a pass.

He went away when we needed him most. We are not sure how we will get through the next four years without him, but this cocktail made in his honor should help.

INGREDIENTS

one cucumber slice, chopped
1 ounce pisco
1 ounce mezcal
pinch of salt
1 ounce vodka
6 ounces lemon-lime soda

1 ounce fresh lemon juice
1 ounce simple syrup
1 large egg white

INSTRUCTIONS

In a cocktail shaker, muddle the cucumber. Add the pisco, mezcal, lemon juice, simple syrup, egg white, instead of a pinch of salt, though, make it with the bitter tears we cried when he retired. Top with lemon-lime soda. Garnish with cucumber slices and a few basil leaves.

SOCIETAL COLLAPSE

I heard, as it were, the sound of thunder. One of the four beasts saying, "come and see." And I saw . . . the recipe for this drink. The original ingredients were pestilence, war, famine, and death, but we've made a few substitutions. Slouch your way toward Bethlehem with this refreshing drink. Pale horse optional.

INGREDIENTS

1 ounce melon liqueur
1 ounce sweet and sour mix   1 ounce blue Curaçao
1 ounce grenadine   1 ounce 151-proof rum

INSTRUCTIONS

Add melon liqueur and sweet and sour mix in a shaker and shake vigorously. Pour mixture into a martini glass. Pour grenadine slowly into the middle of the glass and let it settle into the bottom. Pour rum and blue Curaçao into a shaker and shake vigorously. Over the back of a spoon, slowly float the rum and Curaçao mixture into the glass. This drink can be set on fire, but as we stated before (page 26), the flames may make you feel tingly and uncomfortable. This drink is a Big Bang. Collapse society at your own risk.

> "Societal collapse was always brought about following an advent of the deterioration of marriage and family."
> Mike Pence

Chapter 6

ACCEPTANCE

ac·cept·ance
/ək'septəns/
noun
1) the action of consenting to receive
or undertake something offered.

"We will not accept Donald
Trump as our president."

OR

"We do not accept hate."

WHO IS DRUNK PUBLIUS?

Patient: "Doctor, doctor! You have to help me out. I am deathly afraid of back stories!"
Doctor: "Very interesting. Tell me how this all started."

. . .

Drunk Publius was born under a waning gibbous moon on a balmy November day. Created from the tears of Madison, the dulcet tones of Hamilton, something coughed up by John Jay during an illness, and a generous helping of alcohol, the spirit of Mr. Publius is rumored to stagger out of the fields of the Midwest to protect and mock the Republic when its voters prove to be idiots. If things get really serious, he can merge with Johnny Appleseed, Paul Bunyan, Casey Jones, and Pecos Bill to form a Voltron robot to protect the nation from enemies foreign and domestic.

When not mixing drinks or responding to an existential crisis in America, Drunk Publius enjoys traveling, listening to records, and wrestling bears.

Made in the USA
Middletown, DE
27 July 2017